BUILDING UNIONS

Past, Present and Future

"Who controls the past controls the future; who controls the present controls the past."
George Orwell, 1984

BUILDING UNIONS
PAST, PRESENT AND FUTURE

Author: Peter Kellman
Illustrator: Matt Wuerker

Original Graphic design: Lauren Draper, Corporate Campaign, Inc.
Revised book design by Matthew Tallon

ISBN: 979-8-9898025-7-9

Library of Congress Cataloging-in-Publication Data: Kellman, Peter
1. Labor Unions 2. Working class literature 3. Labor History 4. Constitutional Law 5. Slavery 6. Worker Rights 7. NLRB

Contact Hard Ball Press: hardballpress@gmail.com
415 Argyle Rd., 6A, Brooklyn, NY, 11218

Part 1: THE PROBLEM

The bad news is that in 2025, union membership was down to 9.9%, dropping from a peak of 34% in 1954.[1]

The good news is that given the choice of joining a union or not, 48% of workers in this country would join.

Due to the exportation of jobs, outsourcing production, union-busting and automation, union jobs are being lost as fast as we bring new members in. The strategy of organizing workers worksite by worksite does bring in new members, but employer opposition still denies union representation to millions who want it.

You see the problem. We have to do something different. In Sweden, 83% of the workforce is represented by unions, and employers are prevented by law from interfering with the unionization process. Unlike U.S. workers, Swedish workers have *the right to associate and bargain collectively*. In Sweden, Japan, France, Germany and most other countries with which U.S. corporate managers say we compete, the right to associate and bargain collectively is the law.

The fundamental right to bargain collectively is recognized by the United Nations in the 1948 Declaration of Human Rights under Article 20: "Everyone has the right to freedom of peaceful assembly and association." This right is explained in the UN's International Labor Organization Convention No. 87, *Freedom of Association and the Right to Organize*, which establishes the right of all workers to form and join organizations of their own choosing without prior authorization.

Although 118 countries have ratified Convention No. 87, the U.S. Senate has steadfastly refused to do so.

FREEDOM OF SPEECH + FREEDOM OF ASSEMBLY = FREEDOM OF ASSOCIATION

Suppose a group of people want to form a corporation. They'll call a meeting (freedom of assembly), discuss their options (freedom of speech) and decide they want corporate recognition. Then they'll send a representative to their state capital and file some papers. That's it. Their corporation is recognized by the rest of the society. No cards are signed; no campaign is waged, no one gets fired and there is no election — just recognition. In this country, forming a corporation is a protected activity. But...

Getting a corporation to recognize a union is neither a right nor a protected activity. If it were, 48% of the workforce would *become union members, elect officers and start negotiating contracts in a heartbeat.*

During a union campaign, a U.S. company will put up anti-union posters and hold captive audience meetings. But the union can't put up posters because it doesn't own the walls. The union can't send a representative to the workplace to talk to private-sector workers because the union doesn't own the building.

In this country, we have freedom of speech and assembly only on public property. On private property, the property owners determine who can speak and assemble. Workers surrender their free speech rights to their employers when they enter the workplace.

If we want to associate, to organize, to exercise power, we need to change some fundamental relationships in our society. But first we need to understand how the fundamental relationships that now govern our lives were established.

We need to know our own history.

Part 2: KNOWING OUR HISTORY

"He came to know... that history was not a page in a book, but something held in memory and in blood."[1]

Imagine a church without the Bible, a synagogue without the Torah, a mosque without the Koran or the Iroquois without the Creation Story. It is the teaching of the stories from these great books and oral traditions that holds the congregations and tribes of our people together. The wisdom acquired over the ages is passed down through the stories of the past. These stories guide us into the future. They give us our values, direction and strength. Without them we are rootless, have no direction and live only in the uninformed present.

The same is true for labor. We need a framework to view our history and connect the many stories of our great struggles. We need to learn from our past mistakes and our victories, to take the best from the past and use it to build our future. If we do not, we will forever live in the present and make the same mistakes over and over again.

It is often said in labor circles that we will never increase our numbers until we have

4

better laws. In fact, for most of our history pro-labor laws have been the exception. Most laws relating to labor have been anti-labor and anti-union. It wasn't until 1937 that the National Labor Relations Act was found constitutional. Today, that law is more helpful to employers than it is to us. This is nothing new: the laws were written to favor the wealthy in the 13 American colonies, and it still does in all 50 states today.

ATTACK OF THE FOUNDING FAT CATS

George Washington didn't become one of the wealthiest and most powerful men in America by surveying house lots.[2] It is true that Washington did some surveying for the Ohio Company, in which he was a major stockholder. Washington and other members of the planter and commercial class in colonial Virginia had a plan to exploit labor and make themselves even richer and more powerful. The plan was twofold: first, they would use slaves to run their tobacco plantations, and second, they would create the Ohio Company in 1748.

The company was founded by George's older brother Lawrence and received a grant of 200,000 acres of land west of Virginia from the King of England. Later, Virginia's Royal Governor Dindwiddie, himself an Ohio Company principal, "successfully appealed to the British authorities in London to offer ships passage to indentured servants who would work to clear and improve roads and farmsteads and build company trading posts for seven years, in return for the right to remain on the lands as leaseholders afterward."[3]

Pretty good plan, wasn't it? The King grants the company the land and then supplies unpaid workers to build the roads and the forts to defend it. Then, if the workers survived the passage (and 15% didn't) and their seven years of servitude (and many others didn't), they had the privilege of renting land from the Ohio Company.

But it wasn't just Washington who was involved with this kind of scheme. The Ohio Company competed with the Loyal Land Company of Virginia, owned in part by Thomas Jefferson's dad, and the Vandalia Company, owned in part by Ben Franklin. We have heard a lot about Washington, Jefferson and Franklin, but who were these indentured servants and slaves? What was *their* history?

THIS LAND IS WHOSE LAND?

For our purposes, the history of the indentured servant begins in 1500, when the Roman Catholic Church owned one-third of the land in England, France and Germany. Much of this land was occupied by subsistence farming communities. With the Protestant Reformation of the Church in 1517, Church land was taken over by nobles or sold to speculators, who drove the tenant farmers off the land. Then, in the 1600s and 1700s, the "common lands" which had been available to the poor in Europe were enclosed, fenced off, and the people who lived there driven off the land. Finally, in the 1800s, farmers were pushed off the land they rented to make room for sheep to provide wool for the growing textile industry. This process was known as "clearing the estates."

As the rich stole the best farmland in Europe, they passed laws that called for people

5

WE'RE ALL CREATED EQUAL*

*SOME ARE JUST MORE EQUAL THAN OTHERS

without a place to live or work to be branded, punished, jailed or sold into slavery. That is how a large pool of human beings with an incentive to leave Europe and provide cheap labor in North America was created.

Meanwhile in Africa, rich merchants from Europe organized an international slave trade in which they bought slaves from West African princes whose soldiers were armed with European weapons. The trade in African slaves spanned three centuries. "Before it was over, ten to twelve million Africans would be transported to the New World."[4]

Indentured servants from Europe and slaves from Africa were bought and sold under contract. They provided our founding fathers — men like Washington, Jefferson, Madison and Franklin — with the labor to exploit the natural resources of North America.

> Roughly half the immigrants to colonial America were indentured servants. At the time of the War of Independence, three out of four persons in Pennsylvania, Maryland and Virginia were or had been indentured servants. And by this time, roughly 20 percent of the colonial population was in slavery.[5]

Slaves from Africa and indentured servants from Europe lived under the same fugitive slave laws, and their children were the property of the masters. These people were bought and sold as *property* — a system protected by colonial law and later, by the United States Constitution.

For many of us, the most vivid images of the colonial period are scenes of Thanksgiving, Pocahontas, Captain John Smith and people seeking religious freedom. These images conceal a colonial scenario that went like this: European adventurers "discovered America" and began the process of killing off the indigenous population. They were followed by European speculators who extracted profits from the new land primarily through the labor of African slaves and European indentured servants.

THE AMERICAN "REVOLUTION": INSIDERS AND OUTSIDERS

The American men of property wanted to be free from English taxation and control. In other words, those who made great fortunes on the backs of slaves and indentured servants wanted to be free to exploit the resources of America and not share the wealth with the English ruling class.

The American Revolution was promoted primarily by two groups of people.[6] The members of these two groups had these common characteristics: (1) they owned property; (2) they were white, and (3) they were men.

The first group consisted of speculators, large landowners, plantation owners and those with large commercial interests. In the second group were shopkeepers and skilled artisans, the

small businesspeople of their day. These two groups made up at most 10% of the population. They organized the so-called American revolution and ran the state governments that took power when the 13 colonies declared independence in 1776. They formed the Republic of the United States.

There were more than two groups involved in the revolution. Slaves, free Blacks, indentured servants, freedmen, small farmers, artisans, day laborers, women and Native Americans all played a role, but those who controlled the process were men of great property.

However, most of the population was excluded from participating in the Republic. Those on the outside looking in included people who were the outright property of other people. Some were African slaves and their American descendants, who represented 20% of the population. Another group was indentured servants, people who literally belonged to others for a set period of years. Indentured servants made up about 10% of the population. All women, native people and most freemen without much property were denied the right to vote. In 1787, for example, "every free white man (in South Carolina) of the age of 21...and has a freehold of fifty acres" was eligible to register to vote.[7] To become Governor of South Carolina, the bar was raised even higher: one was required to be worth 10,000 pounds.[8]

ENGLAND RULES ENSLAVED PERSONS MAY GO FREE

Washington and the other wealthy landowners had an additional reason to want to break from the British Kingdom: An English court had ruled that Somerset James, an enslaved man brought by his master from the colonies to London, could refuse passage back to the Americas and was, fundamentally, a free man. He could choose to work for his prior "owner" or seek employment elsewhere.

News that the English courts were not recognizing ownership of another human being in England spread rapidly across the colonies. At the same time, anti-slavery members of Parliament were threatening to bring a bill that would outlaw slavery in the colonies (with reparations paid in full to...the slave owners).

Facing these threats to their "property" rights, the wealthy elites drummed up support for the rebellion against the Crown, never mentioning their real motives. They were not interested in changing the balance of power in their new country. They were happy to keep on exploiting labor and natural resources. Their war for independence was not a revolution, it was merely the exchange of a royal, hereditary ruling class of England for the wealthy, landowners and merchants of the new colonies.

New rulers, same old tiny minority owning those who labor.

THE CONSTITUTION: BUSINESS AS USUAL

In 1781, the former colonies, now states, ratified a set of rules called the Articles of Confederation, which determined their relationship to each other. In 1787, the state legislatures sent delegates to a meeting to discuss amending the Articles of Confederation. This meeting was the Constitutional Convention of 1787, held in Philadelphia. It was a closed meeting, the minutes of which were made public 53 years later.[9]

Much had happened between 1781 and 1787 that caused the class of people who fomented the revolution to be concerned about their future. Divisions within the propertied class surfaced in the state legislatures, and conflict between classes manifested itself in armed insurrections against the authority of state governments.

In the legislatures, conflicts arose between small business owners and artisans and those involved in national and international trade. The small businessmen wanted high state tariffs to protect their small concerns, while those with large commercial interests demanded so-called "free trade" between the states.

Meanwhile, the people who were clearing the land wanted to own it, and armed insurrection against state authority broke out in many places. For example, the rebellion of Vermont's Green Mountain Boys against their New York landlords eventually led to the establishment of Vermont as the 14th State in 1777. But it was Shays Rebellion, the 1786-87 armed insurrection of western Massachusetts farmers against the policies of the commercial class in Boston, that weighed most heavily upon the large property owners who sat down in 1787 to write the Constitution of the United States. Those who wanted free trade between the states saw the need to have a strong federal government as well as a federal army that would always be available to put down rebellions that could not be suppressed by state militias.

The men who assembled in Philadelphia in 1787 to write the Constitution were all men of property. The noted historian Charles Beard states that James Madison, primary author of the Constitution, "in more than one speech pointed out that the conflict of interests was inescapable. He told the convention that *the greatest conflict of all in the country was between those who had property and those who had none.*"[10]

9

Participants were pledged to secrecy, but James Madison's notes were made public in 1840.

Beard also wrote: "Leaders among the framers wanted, among other things, first to hold the Union together; second, to set up a government that would protect, regulate, and promote types of economic enterprise; third, to put brakes on the state legislatures which had been attacking the interests of protected classes."[11] *Here is some of what the founding fathers came up with.*

THE COMMERCE CLAUSE: THE FIRST NAFTA

The Commerce Clause of the Constitution, Article 1, Sec. 8 [3], was written "to regulate Commerce with foreign Nations, and among the several States, and with the Indian Tribes." After the Constitution was ratified, independent state legislatures were no longer able to erect protective tariffs that "hindered" the flow of goods between the states. The big commercial interests of the day had triumphed over the small enterprises trying to "grow" local businesses.

Recently, a similar event took place when large transnational corporate interests triumphed over national business interests and labor with the passage of the North American Free Trade Agreement (NAFTA). The Commerce Clause was the first "free trade" agreement in North America, and like NAFTA, it was negotiated at a closed meeting.

THE CONTRACTS CLAUSE: HERE IT IS, MYTH AMERICA.

The Contracts Clause of the Constitution, Article 1 Sec. 10, states in part: "No State shall...pass any...Law impairing the Obligation of contracts." Legal theory holds that contracts are agreements made between equals, and therefore the state should not meddle. If a state were to pass a *public* law that, for example, set the maximum hours an employer can require people to work, it would be seen by the courts as *impairing* the right of individual citizens to negotiate contracts free from outside interference.

A private contract is not technically a "law" itself, but rather an agreement between individuals that is governed by contract law. Contract law is itself a branch of private law. This means that the terms of the contract create legally binding obligations between the parties involved. The contract is enforceable by the legal system if one of the parties fails to meet their contractual obligations.

Thus, most labor laws passed by state legislatures and Congress prior to 1937 were ruled unconstitutional by the U.S. Supreme Court because they violated the Contracts Clause. They were *public laws* that violated *private laws*.

The meaning is clear: the obligation of the government, as stated in the Preamble to the Constitution, to promote the "general welfare" is secondary to the *private* law, the law of contracts.

Once again, the theory of contracts is based on the assumption that the contracting parties are equals. The founding fathers would have us believe that an indentured servant negotiating a contract with his master was somehow equal to the master at the negotiating table. The situation is similar to a small local union with 200 members negotiating a contract with a large employer who brings to the table enough resources to move the plant. In practice, this can hardly be called a contract negotiated between equals. But this is the legal fiction, and the courts, Congress, National Guard, army and police uphold this distortion of common sense.

The *Lochner v. New York* case (1905) is a classic example of how the Contracts Clause suppressed the democratic legislative activities of working class people. As a result of popular agitation, the New York State Legislature passed a law limiting the hours of work for people employed in bakeries to no more than 10 per day and 60 per week. The U.S. Supreme Court ruled, "Under such circumstances the freedom of master and employee to contract with each other in relation to their employment, and in defining the same, cannot be prohibited or interfered with, without violating the Federal Constitution."

Laws found constitutional today limiting the hours a person can work are generally found applying to children and situations in which public safety would be affected by tired workers, as in the railroad or trucking industries.

Dominance of the *private* law over the *public* law in our Constitution has made it very hard for working people to use the political process to improve their conditions. This is true because the Constitution restricts our collective activity primarily to contractual relationships with employers, and the National Labor Relations Act serves to limit our activity even further. So much for "We the People" forming a Government to "promote the general Welfare," as promised in the Preamble.

But who defines the "general Welfare?" So far, it has been the lawyers of the elite who become Supreme Court justices — not shop stewards, teachers or homemakers. When the constitutionality of a law is questioned, it is five Supreme Court justices who decide for the rest of us issues like: Is a maximum 40-hour week constitutional? Do workers have free speech rights at work? Do employers have free speech rights in union certification elections? In a close election, such as Tilden *vs.* Hayes in 1887 or Bush *vs.* Gore in 2000, who becomes President?

'RETURN SERVANTS' CLAUSE: YOU BELONG TO ME

Human rights didn't seem to be high on the agenda of the Constitution's framers, but labor did make it into the Constitution (Article 4, Sec. 2. [3]):

> No person held in Service or Labour in one State, under the laws thereof, escaping into another, shall, in Consequence of any regulation therein, be discharged from such Service or Labour, but shall be delivered up on Claim of the Party to whom such Service or Labour may be due.

Men like Madison and Washington wanted their human property, slaves and indentured servants, to know that if they escaped into another state, the Constitution of the United States guaranteed their return. Madison, our fourth President and "master builder of the Constitution," had a great financial interest in protecting his property. He "told a British visitor shortly after the American Revolution that he could make $257 on every Negro in a year, and spend only

$12 or $13 on his keep."

At one time James Madison enslaved 116 human beings. Based on his statement, Madison would have made a yearly profit of $28,304 on slave labor, and the slaves would have realized nothing but the inhumanity of being a slave. If you were a slave or indentured servant, how would you feel about this "master builder of the Constitution" writing *your* constitution?

THE FIRST AMENDMENT: DID YOU SAY 'PRIVATIZE?'

In order to get the Constitution ratified by the states, the framers promised that after it took effect they would support amendments to address the many complaints voiced against it. One of the promised amendments that made it into the Constitution is the one we know today as the First Amendment. Passed in 1791, it guaranteed freedom of speech and assembly and was heralded as a great step forward for democracy. Workers today are still awaiting the fulfillment of its promise.

The First Amendment is commonly believed to guarantee us freedom of the press, speech and assembly. As we know, the reality today is that freedom of the press only applies to those who own the press. As for freedom of speech and assembly, what the Constitution actually guarantees is: "Congress shall make no law...abridging the freedom of speech, or the press; or the right of the people peaceably to assemble."

Let us be clear here: when the Constitution says "Congress shall make no law," it means there will be no *public* law denying people free speech. But what about the *private* law? The Constitution does *not* say that employers cannot deny workers freedom of speech and assembly. It speaks to what the Congress will *not* do; it does not speak to what *people who own property* will not do.

In other words, if we want freedom of speech, assembly and association, we need to amend the First Amendment to say: *Congress shall guarantee the people's right to freedom of religion, the press, speech, assembly and association. These rights and the government's responsibility to promote the General Welfare and Human Rights shall take precedence over all other matters.*

So labor got the shaft. But how did corporations, the agencies of today's propertied class, get constitutional protection and support?

Part 3: CORPORATIONS AND THE CONSTITUTION

A FIGHT OVER PUBLIC SCHOOLS

In 1816, small property owners and skilled artisans who believed in Thomas Jefferson's vision of a republican form of government were elected in such numbers that they became the majority in the New Hampshire Legislature and elected one of their own as governor.

The basis of Jeffersonian republicanism was a society primarily composed of small farmers. An important component of republican philosophy was that it required educated people to insure a republican form of government. These people wanted to know that higher education would be available for their children.

However, colleges during that period were mainly private schools, like Yale, Harvard and Dartmouth — holdovers from the colonial days. These schools were linked to the past by class and religion. They were by design not republican in nature. Their original purpose was to spread the word of Christianity in support of the British Empire and to educate the children of the elite.

Dartmouth College was chartered by the King of England in 1769 as an Indian Charity School "with a view to spreading the knowledge of the great Redeemer among their savage tribes."[1]

APPLYING "EQUAL PROTECTION"

Of the cases in this court in which the 14ᵀᴴ Amendment was applied during the first fifty years after its adoption, less than one half of one percent invoked it in protection of the Negro race, and more than fifty percent asked that its benefits be extended to corporations.
— Justice Hugo Black

AFRICAN AMERICANS   CORPORATIONS

It soon evolved into a school "to promote learning among the English, and be a means to supply a great number of churches...with a learned and orthodox ministry."[2]

The college was a cog in the colonialist machine that supported and promoted the British Empire.

Led by Jeffersonian republicans, a national movement developed after the revolution to turn the colonial colleges into public (or publicly responsible) schools. In New Hampshire, the movement took the form of "An Act To Amend The Charter And Enlarge And Improve The Corporation of Dartmouth College." The text of the law, passed in 1816, begins, "Whereas knowledge and learning generally diffused through a Community are essential to the preservation of free Government, and extending the opportunities and advantages of education is highly conducive to promote this end," the legislature made *private* Dartmouth College into *public* Dartmouth University and ordered it to set up colleges around the state. New Hampshire Gov. William Plumer promoted the change, arguing that the original provisions of Dartmouth College "emanated from royalty and contained principles...hostile to the spirit and genius of free government."

The trustees of Dartmouth objected to the charter change and took the state to court.

The state Supreme Court ruled in favor of the legislature, arguing that it had the right to change the charter of the college "...because it is a matter of too great moment, too intimately connected with the public welfare and prosperity, to be thus entrusted in the hands of a few. The education of the rising generation is a matter of the highest public concerns, and is worthy of the best attention of every legislature." The decision was appealed to the U.S. Supreme Court, which reversed the state court *and gave the corporate form a constitutional life*.[3]

The U.S. Supreme Court wasn't interested in promoting public education. The Court was set up to be the final protector of a propertied class, and it delivered, ruling that a corporation is a *private* contract, not a *public* law. The Court decreed that although the state created the corporation when it issued the charter, it is not *sovereign* over that charter but is simply a *party* to the contract.[4] All of which means that the corporation is protected from many forms of state interference by the Contracts Clause of the Constitution. And Dartmouth University, a *public* school, once again became a *private* college.

The Dartmouth decision of 1819 established the principle that corporations get constitutional protection because they are *private* contracts with the state.

In 1886, the U.S. Supreme Court ruled (*Santa Clara v. Southern Pacific Railroad*) that corporations also have the constitutional shield of "equal protection" as *persons* under the 14th Amendment. This means that corporations are recognized constitutionally (by the Dartmouth College case), and on top of that, corporate activity has 14th Amendment "equal protection" (Santa Clara case). In other words, corporations gained significant constitutional protections at a time, 1886, when most flesh-and-blood persons — women, Native Americans and most African-Americans — were *denied* the right to vote, and therefore *denied* equal protection.

If you have any doubts about the role the courts have played in advancing the pre-eminence of the property rights of the propertied class over the human rights of the working class, consider these facts:

- The 14th Amendment states, "No state shall make or enforce any law which shall abridge the privileges or immunities of citizens of the United States; nor shall any State deprive any *person* of life, liberty, or property, without due process of law; nor deny any *person* within its jurisdiction the equal protection of the laws" (emphasis added). The 14th Amendment was added to the Constitution in 1868 to protect the rights of freed slaves, but as Supreme Court Justice Hugo Black pointed out in *Connecticut General v. Johnson* (1938), "Of the cases in this court in which the Fourteenth Amendment was applied during the first fifty years after its adoption, less than one-half of one percent invoked it in protection of the Negro race, and more than fifty percent asked that its benefits be extended to corporations."
- In *Minor v. Happersett* (1875)[4], women from Ohio argued that under the 14th Amendment protection of due process, the U.S. Constitution established that their right to vote could not be denied by the state. The U.S. Supreme Court rejected that argument. Women received constitutional protection

for the right to vote 48 years later in 1920, when the 19th Amendment established that the right to vote could not be denied on the basis of sex and that Congress shall have the power to enforce the Amendment by passing appropriate legislation.

- While the courts were extending "rights" to corporate persons and denying them to women, by 1920 the courts had struck down roughly 300 labor laws.[5]
- More than 1,800 injunctions against strikes were issued between 1880 and 1931.[6] Of the 118 labor injunctions heard in federal courts between 1901 and 1928, 70 of them were issued *ex parte*, i.e. without giving the defendants the opportunity to be heard because they were not even notified of the hearing. Of course, *all* the defendants in these cases were labor unions.

It appears that the Supreme Court has two sides to its brain. With one side it creates, protects and promotes "rights" for the institutions of the rich. With the other side it suppresses human rights, such as the right to vote and the right to associate.

THREE PEOPLE'S MOVEMENTS

One of the reasons the framers of the Constitution created a federal government was to protect themselves from those who also wanted to be included in "We the People." By the 1830s, movements were emerging to end slavery, advance the cause of labor and extend equal rights to women. All slavery was ended after the Civil War with the passage of the 13th Amendment in 1865 ("Neither slavery nor involuntary servitude...shall exist within the United States..."). The struggle for women's suffrage culminated with the passage of the 19th Amendment in 1920 ("The right of citizens of the United States to vote shall not be denied or abridged by the United States or by any State on account of sex").

With the passage of these amendments and the continuing agitation by the people who put them in the Constitution, major changes have taken place in our society. Restrictions on voter registration relating to property, sex and race are largely gone (for the moment), and both women and people of color *with* property now have access to due process, although that "due process" is not always extended to undocumented immigrants.

Perhaps the most important achievements of the movements for sexual and racial equality were getting the story of their struggles into schoolbooks and creating academic departments dedicated to the study and promotion of these movements' goals — a victory now sadly being attacked and eroded in school districts across the country.

However, labor has yet to make it into the Constitution, because the one concession that a propertied class will resist the hardest is one that would lead to a redistribution of wealth and power.

The goals of the 1830s labor movement — the ten-hour workday and public education — focused on democracy. Labor people argued that if they were to build a democracy, they had to be educated, and to be educated they needed time to go to school. So they fought for the ten-hour day and free public education, not as benefits in and of themselves but as conditions necessary to bring about a republican form of government.

The labor movement of the 1830s had picked up the ball hit by the New Hampshire Legislature in 1816 — a ball declared foul by the U.S. Supreme Court in the Dartmouth case of 1819. In promoting legislation to make Dartmouth College a public university, the Governor of New Hampshire has said that private education, "emanated from royalty and contained principles...hostile to the spirit and genius of free government."

In support of the New Hampshire Legislature, the state Supreme Court stated: '...because it is a matter of too great moment, too intimately connected with the public welfare and prosperity, to be thus entrusted in the hands of a few. The education of the rising generation is a matter of the highest public concerns, and is worthy of the best attention of every legislature."

DEMOCRACY DAY: PEOPLE GET READY

If the insights of the 1830s labor movement were applied today, we would link hours of work to the present lack of democracy and call for a work week composed of four eight-hour days and a fifth day to participate in creating a democracy: "Democracy Day." Because

we understand that there is more to democracy than just voting every few years, we need to have the time to participate in the functioning of government. So one day a week would be set aside, in the language of the 1830s, for the "*common* people" to study and participate in the functioning of a democratic government. On that day every week, they would sit on local boards and participate in public meetings and seminars. The corporate lobbyists would be shaking and quaking if millions of working-class people had the time to actually participate in the legislative process — time to, as unionists said in the 1890s, "perfect our organization."

While working people struggled to "perfect our organization," the propertied class found a vehicle to perfect *its* organization: the corporation.

CORPORATE RESPONSIBILITY

Only a few corporations were chartered just after the revolution, and their activities were narrowly defined by the legislatures that chartered them. For example, a corporation chartered to build a turnpike couldn't be used to make textiles. A corporation chartered to make textiles couldn't build a turnpike. Nor could a turnpike or textile corporation own other companies. Furthermore, the stockholders of corporations were not insulated from the liabilities of the corporation the way managers and stockholders are today. That is, the stockholders of a corporation chartered in 1800 were individually responsible for the corporation's debts and liable for its acts.

Translated into today's world, this would mean that corporate managers would be personally responsible for corporate violations of law, and stockholders would pay the debts of a corporation that declared bankruptcy. An individual today who violates a serious labor or environmental law will go to jail.

But how do you put a corporation in jail? In 1800, the charter would be revoked.

Now *that's* corporate responsibility!

Even today, the corporation's Achilles heel is its charter. "We the people" elect representatives to our state legislatures. These legislatures have the power to issue, revise and revoke charters. Maybe it's time for labor to put the "revise-and-revoke" language on our legislative agenda when the policies of particular corporations run counter to the human rights of workers.

In 1800, the rich held their property primarily as individuals who owned so many acres of land, slaves or businesses. But by the end of the Civil War, the propertied class had shifted its mode of exercising power from the individual to the corporation.

1876: RAILROADING AN ELECTION

By the 1870s, the railroad corporations were literally running the country. When the outcome of the 1876 presidential election was disputed, the decision was left to a special commission composed of five Supreme Court justices and 10 congressmen. Ostensibly, this group was to choose either Democrat Samuel J. Tilden or Republican Rutherford B. Hayes to serve as President of the United States. But labor historian Philip Foner tells what really happened:

> The actual determination was made by Thomas A. Scott, president of the Pennsylvania Railroad, who, in return for assurances of support for a Texas Pacific Railroad, obtained the votes of the southern congressmen for Hayes. It is hardly an accident that on March 2, 1877, when Hayes received the telegram confirming his election, he was *en route* to Washington in Tom Scott's own luxurious private car.[7]

For our purposes, it matters little that the election was bought by a railroad CEO. What matters is the impact that the Hayes administration had on the lives of freed slaves, union labor and the generations of Americans that followed. In fact, the present-day status of African-Americans and the labor movement was significantly affected by two actions that Hayes took as president. First, he ended Reconstruction by pulling out the last of the federal troops who were in the South to ensure equal rights and a new start for freed slaves. Second, he used federal troops to end the great labor uprising of 1877 in which more than 100 strikers were killed. Jeremy Brecher begins the story:

> In the centers of many American cities are positioned huge armories, grim nineteenth-century edifices of brick and stone. They are fortresses, complete with massive walls and loopholes for guns. You may have wondered why they are there, but it never occurred to you that they were built to protect America not against invasion from abroad but against popular revolt at home. Their erection was a monument to the Great Upheaval of 1877.[8]

In July of 1877, in the midst of a depression, railroad workers struck in response to grossly unsafe working conditions and repeated pay cuts. Their strike shut down the industry. As it spread, workers in other industries joined, and the rail strike became a general strike in a dozen major cities. In April, President Hayes had withdrawn the last of the federal troops from the South. In July, he sent them into battle against labor. Then in the fall, federal troops fought the Sioux Indians.

How different would the country be if the federal government in 1877 had been run by the people instead of the CEO of a railroad corporation? Suppose federal troops had been used to *protect* labor, freed slaves and Native Americans in 1877, rather than suppressing them? And just think: if shop stewards served on the Supreme Court instead of lawyers, the history of labor injunctions would be the history of corporate injunctions.

Part 4: LABOR STANDS UP

THE RISE OF THE KNIGHTS

After the 1877 upheaval was put down by federal troops, Labor resurfaced with the rise of the Knights of Labor, whose membership reached one million by 1886. In place of corporations and the wage labor system, the Knights called for the establishment of "co-operative institutions such as will tend to supersede the wage system, by the introduction of [a] co-operative industrial system."

The Knights fought for a shorter workday by advocating a general refusal to work more than eight hours a day. They sought the creation of producer, consumer and distributive cooperatives; the prohibition of child labor; equal pay for equal work regardless of race or gender, and universal suffrage. The Knights opposed the concentration of wealth and power in the hands of a few.

African-Americans played an important role in the Knights of Labor:

> When workers in Richmond, Virginia, hosted the Order's 1886 General Assembly, the racist southern press did not miss the opportunity to castigate the Knights' interracial delegations, pointing, with particular horror, to the mixing in public of white and black men and women... But the organization stood its ground on the race question. The city's African-American workers responded by treating visiting Knights to a huge labor parade.[1]

The Knights believed the working class should exercise power through the ballot and the boycott. They urged the settlement of labor disputes by arbitration. Employers who were unwilling to settle through arbitration were subjected to massive community boycotts. The American Federation of Labor was created by trade unions that split from the Knights in 1886. Soon afterward the AFL became the "union of unions," or labor federation, that it is today.

INTANGIBLE PROPERTY: DOES THE NON-BUYER CONSPIRE?

The successes Labor achieved through the Knights and the early AFL were due in part to boycotts, in which large numbers of people urged others not to do something, like shop at a store, work or buy a product. A boycott is an example of the exercise of free speech. But when boycotts began hurting the propertied class, the courts, in the role assigned to them by the framers, responded. Labor historian Charles Scontras states:

> It was perfectly legal for an individual to strike, picket, or boycott, and the employers had no legal recourse for injury suffered from such activities of an individual. It was necessary, therefore, to show that union actions such as strikes, boycotts, and picketing were

illegal activities. To achieve this end, courts began to revive the old common law of conspiracy. While the old conspiracy doctrine held that conspiracy was a crime because it threatened the public, the new interpretation of conspiracy held that it was a civil offense because it threatened irreparable damage to intangible property. Thus, it was no longer necessary for employers to show that irreparable damage to tangible property would result if such activities took place, but only to show that irreparable damage would occur against intangible property rights to do business and realize a profit.[2]

Future corporate profits come under the definition of intangible property. But what about wages? When was the last time you heard of an injunction being issued against an employer for refusing to negotiate in good faith? Doesn't that activity interfere with a worker's future earnings? How is that any different from interfering with the future earnings of a business? Have you ever heard of a CEO being put in jail to prevent him from taking actions that might jeopardize the future earnings of workers employed by his company?

LABOR INJUNCTIONS

John Mitchell, president of the Mine Workers Union, said in 1903: "No weapon has been used with such disastrous effects against trade unions as has the injunction." [3]

Historically, *injunctive* law has been utilized against labor by employers with the help of more-than-willing judges.

Court activity is usually based on some action that has already taken place, and the court rules as to whether or not the activity was in violation of some existing law. With an injunction the court forbids, or *enjoins,* a future activity. (Between 1880 and 1931, judges issued 1800 injunctions against strikes.) To enforce the injunction, the judge can levy fines and send people to jail. If you violate an injunction, the

judge will find you in contempt of court. That is, the judge finds that you violated not a law written by a legislature, but a law created by the judge.

What we have here is the court deciding that the liberty of workers to engage in collective activity (boycotting, striking or picketing) is a lesser liberty than that of an employer to engage in business. This means, for example, that the court has the power to jail people who simply *advocate* that people not buy a product.

'THE LABOR AMENDMENT'

The 13th Amendment, passed after the Civil War, states in Section 1, "Neither slavery nor involuntary servitude...shall exist within the United States," and in Section 2, "Congress shall have the power to enforce this article by appropriate legislation." Many workers believed this language applied to them and called it "the labor amendment."

They believed that freedom meant the abolition of the condition of involuntary servitude both on and off the job. They reasoned that it was Congress's responsibility to make the amendment a reality in working-class life. They argued that denial of freedom of speech, assembly and organization on the job, or of the right to strike and boycott, was tantamount to involuntary servitude.

To those who said workers were free to quit their jobs, they replied that the same conditions applied on almost every job a laborer might obtain in the Industrial Age, and therefore, the right to quit was virtually meaningless as long as one needed a job to survive. As Samuel Gompers, the first president of the AFL, said, "The only workers not laboring under terms and conditions arbitrarily imposed upon them from a source wholly foreign to themselves, are the organized workers." [4]

The courts, with few exceptions, found no merit in the "labor amendment" argument and consistently took the corporations' side. They routinely enjoined strikes, picket lines and boycotts. Yet in 1908 it became the official policy of the American Federation of Labor that a union confronted with an unconstitutional injunction had an "imperative duty" to "refuse obedience and take whatever consequences might ensue."[5]

TOTAL U.S. UNION MEMBERSHIP 1900-2024		
Year	Union Members	Residential Population
1900	932,000	76,094,000
1905	1,947,000	83,822,000
1910	2,168,000	92,822,000
1915	2,598,000	100,546,000
1920	4,823,000	106,461,000
1925	3,685,000	115,829,000
1930	3,750,000	123,077,000
1935	3,649,000	127,250,000
1940	7,296,000	132,457,000
1945	12,254,000	133,434,000
1950	14,294,000	151,868,000
1955	16,127,000	165,000,000
1960	15,516,000	180,000,000
1965	18,269,000	194,000,000
1970	20,990,000	204,000,000
1975	22,207,000	215,000,000
1980	20,969,000	227,000,000
1985	16,996,000	238,000,000
1990	16,740,000	249.000,000
1995	16,360,000	263,000,000
2000	16,300,000	276,000,000
2005	15,700,000	296,842,670
2010	14,700,000	311,182,845
2015	14,800,000	324,607,776
2020	14,250,000	335,942,003
2024	14,400,000	341,814,420

WORLD WAR I: LABOR ON A LEASH

In 1917 and 1918, government support of workers in war-related industries was in sync with official propaganda promoting political democracy abroad. While the federal government supported industrial democracy at home, labor organizations that supported the war increased their membership and influence.

In order to prevent labor-management disputes from curtailing war-related production, President Woodrow Wilson created the War Labor Board. This board conducted workplace elections to decide which *workers* (not which unions) would form workplace councils. The Board arbitrated disagreements between these councils and management. If a corporation wouldn't go along with a decision, Wilson used his wartime powers to nationalize the corporation. On the other hand, if workers failed to abide by a Board ruling, the president sent in the troops.

Although the War Labor Board didn't promote unions *per se*, the reality was that union members ran for the worker-representative positions — and invariably won because they represented the best organized part of the workforce. Hence, as union power increased, so did union membership.

The democracy advocated by the United States government during the war was hollow. When Congress declared war in 1917, it effectively abolished free speech by enacting the Espionage Act, which made it a crime to say anything that would "discourage" enlistment in the armed forces. The American Federation of Labor supported the war and its unions flourished.

However, leaders and members of the Industrial Workers of the World (the "Wobblies") expressed opposition to the war. They were harassed and jailed, and as a result, their union was seriously weakened. One of the jailed Wobblies was Ralph Chaplin, who wrote the lyrics to Labor's anthem "Solidarity Forever." While in jail, Chaplin wrote a book of poems called "Bars and Shadows." In the introduction, economist Scott Nearing explained why the Wobblies were singled out for persecution:

> Long before the war, the I.W.W. had made itself known and feared for its conduct of strikes; its free speech fights, and its ability to put the sore spots of American industrial life on the front pages of the daily press... It was in the domain of industry that the I.W.W. was functioning, and it was among the business interests that the determination had been reached to rid the country of the organization at all costs.[6]

The best-known of the thousands jailed for violating the Espionage Act was labor leader Eugene V. Debs, who helped organize the American Railway Union and had been jailed earlier for leading the Pullman strike of 1894. Debs was sentenced to ten years in federal prison under the Espionage Act for making anti-war speeches.[7]

That being said, the war years of 1917-18 were both good and bad for unions. The working class was empowered by the unions' call for industrial democracy here and by the government's call to "make the world safe for democracy" over there. And President Wilson would not allow the corporate managers to wage war against workers who belonged to unions that went along with the war.

However, once the war ended, all bets were off. The corporate managers declared war on the unions. This time the government enlisted on management's side, and with the IWW out of the way, the AFL unions took it on the chin.

LABOR CRUSHED: THE 'AMERICAN PLAN'

After the war, the Iron Heel of big business moved to crush the growing movement for industrial democracy. (The Iron Heel is the title of a 1906 book by Jack London in which he portrays a workers' revolt crushed by the employers.) The corporate managers of that period wanted to put in place the "American Plan," which called for the open shop, where workers are not required to join the union or pay union dues. The wealthy business owners advocated company-run welfare institutions, company-run social institutions and company-controlled local governments. To make it work, the unions had to be destroyed.

When the captains of industry called for huge reductions in wages, the unions were forced to strike. Using "government by injunction," the strikes were crushed. Meanwhile, U.S. Attorney General A. Mitchell Palmer was rounding up, detaining and extraditing foreign-born union activists.

Sacco and Vanzetti were framed, tried and executed. Most anyone who dared challenge the corporate elites was tried and convicted in the press and often, by the courts. The harshest treatment of all was meted out to African-Americans: between 1918 and 1921, 28 people were publicly burned alive by mobs, and in 1932, at least 24 were lynched.

Some historians refer to this period as the "Little Red Scare," but there was nothing little about it. Hundreds of union activists were deported, killed and jailed, and tens of thousands were blacklisted. By 1933, union membership fell to 5.4% of the civilian labor force.

In all previous depressions in the U.S., labor union membership had declined, but as the Great Depression deepened, labor started to come back, as unorganized workers knocked on the union door in unprecedented numbers. Workers who had been suffering in silence during the 1920s were once again on the move.

Part 5: LABOR WINS AND LOSES

NORRIS-LAGUARDIA AND FREEDOM OF ASSOCIATION

As we have seen, from 1901 through 1928, federal courts issued 118 labor injunctions of which 70 were granted on the basis of employer affidavits without labor even having the opportunity to be heard.[1]

By 1932 the country was tired of "government by injunction" and the Republican Senate and the Democratic House passed the Norris-LaGuardia Anti-Injunction Act, which was signed by Republican President Herbert Hoover. This Anti-Injunction Act outlawed the "yellow dog contract" and stated in Section 1 that "No court of the United States...shall have jurisdiction to issue restraining or temporary or permanent injunctions in a case involving or growing out of a labor dispute, except in a strict conformity with the provisions of this Act."[2] In Section 2, Congress described the existing relationship between labor and the owners of property in the United States:

> Whereas under prevailing economic conditions, developed with the aid of governmental authority for owners of property to organize in the corporate and other forms of ownership association, the individual unorganized worker is commonly helpless to exercise actual liberty of contract and to protect his freedom of labor, and thereby to obtain acceptable terms and conditions of employment...

Congress went on to lay out the solution:

> ...it is necessary that he have full freedom of association, self organization, and designation of representatives of his own choosing, to negotiate the terms and conditions of his employment, and that he shall be free from the interference, restraint, or coercion of employers of labor, or their agents, in the designation of such representatives or in self organization or in other concerted activities for the purpose of collective bargaining or other mutual aid or protection; therefore, the following definitions of and limitations upon the jurisdiction and authority of the courts of the United States are enacted.

In one legislative act the injunction was lifted off labor's back, the yellow dog contract was abolished and a worker could now enjoy, as the act stated, *"full freedom of association...and that he shall be free from the interference, restraint, or coercion of employers of labor...in self organization or in other concerted activities for the purpose of collective bargaining or other mutual aid or protection."*

Labor now had its Magna Charta. Freedom of association was the law. The American Federation of Labor's goal — a law recognizing the right of workers to freely associate — had been achieved. Labor could organize, boycott and strike, and employers could no longer rely on the federal courts for injunctions or police interference on their behalf. [3]

THE NEW DEAL AND THE NLRA

Despite this legislative victory, not much changed. It was 1932, labor was weak and employers still held most of the cards. President Franklin D. Roosevelt launched the New Deal the following year. It included the establishment of a labor board, but more importantly, the administration supported union organizing as a way to help the country climb out of the Depression. The purpose of Roosevelt's labor board (and shortly thereafter, the National Labor Relations Board) was to cut down on strikes, which hurt production. However, unions *were* encouraged because Roosevelt believed that as more workers were organized, wages would go up. Workers would have more money to spend on goods, more goods would be produced and the country would "grow" its way out of the Depression (the opposite of trickle-down economics, or what you might call "trickle-up").

However, many of Roosevelt's programs were found unconstitutional until he threatened to "stack" or enlarge the Supreme Court. The National Labor Relations Act of 1935 was found constitutional in *NLRB v. Jones & Laughlin Steel Corp.* (1937). The court's opinion reflected the language of the Norris-LaGuardia Anti-Injunction Act:

> Employees have as clear a right to organize and select their representatives for lawful purposes as the respondent has to organize its business and select its own officers and agents. Discrimination and coercion to prevent the free exercise of the right of employees to self organization and representation is a proper subject for condemnation by competent legislative authority. Long ago we stated the reason for labor organizations. We said that they were organized out of the necessities of the situation; that a single employee was helpless in dealing with an employer; that he was dependent ordinarily on his daily wage for the maintenance of himself and family; that, if the employer refused to pay him the wages that he thought fair, he was nevertheless unable to leave the employ and resist arbitrary and unfair treatment; that union was essential to give laborers opportunity to deal on an equality with their employer.

Furthermore, the Norris-LaGuardia Anti-Injunction Act passed constitutional muster in February of 1938. This meant that workers were free to organize and strike; boycotts were legal, and permanent replacements were illegal. It meant that the yellow dog contract and the dreaded labor injunction were history. Despite these significant labor victories, large employers like General Motors and U.S. Steel weren't going to automatically recognize unions. Having the government out of the way was one thing, but having the government on your side was another. So workers were forced on their own to shut down entire cities with general strikes and take over factories in order to gain employer recognition.

ADVANCES AND OBSTACLES

As the Depression dragged on, workers continued to organize and their power increased to the point that Roosevelt was beholden to labor for his re-election to the presidency in 1936. Labor had become so strong that when workers took over the General Motors Corporation factory in Flint, Michigan, late in 1936, neither the governor of the state nor the President sent troops to remove the strikers from the corporation's property. The strikers won and 18 sit-downs followed at other GM facilities, culminating in union recognition.

But in May of 1938, the Court took a big step backward in *NLRB v. Mackay Radio*, ruling that permanent replacement of strikers was legal; thus, the right to strike became little more than the right to quit. The Court went on in *NLRB v. Virginia Electric & Power* (1941) to grant free speech rights to employers in union certification elections. [4]

In 1947, Congress passed the Taft-Hartley "Slave Labor" Act, which created the Taft-Hartley injunction. That injunction allowe the President to set in motion injunctions against "national emergency strikes" that "imperil the national health or safety," thus nullifying the gains made under Norris-LaGuardia. Taft-Hartley:

- allowed state legislatures to ban the union shop.
- outlawed the closed shop.
- made sympathy strikes and secondary boycotts illegal for all practical purposes.
- barred from participating in NLRB elections unions that didn't ban Communists from their membership.
- took away union control of pension funds and health and welfare funds.
- allowed *employers* the right to actively and vocally oppose having labor unions in their enterprises.
- forced foremen out of the unions.
- created the decertification election.

Unions increased membership as a percentage of the workforce from 5.4% in 1933 to 25.7% in 1953. [5]

For two brief periods in our history, the government was helpful to Labor: 1917-18 (War Labor Board) and 1937-47 (the National Labor Relations Act prior to Taft-Hartley). In 2001, union membership hovered around 13.5%.[6]

Along with the sharp decline in union economic and political power has come an erosion in the standard of living for most workers, whose real wages peaked in 1973.

PART 6: LABOR'S FUTURE

If the news for labor has been bad, it hasn't been *all* bad. Because the abolition, suffrage and labor movements took seriously the words "We the People" from the Preamble to the Constitution, chattel slavery is no more. All citizens — not just white males with property — can *in theory* vote, regardless of race, sex or ownership of property. Those rights are written amendments to the Constitution.

Unfortunately, the old anti-labor, anti-human rights forces have succeeded in eroding voting rights in many states. They have set up barriers to registering to vote, challenged huge blocks of voters, and instituted other measures that make it more difficult for many citizens — especially people of color and immigrants — to cast their votes.

A number of the legislative goals sought by the labor movement since the 1830s, like the laws protecting children in the workplace and providing health and safety protection for workers and free public education, remain in effect, although even they are meeting challenges from right wing legislators.

The right to *free association* (which includes the right to organize, strike and boycott) has been relegated to the back burner. However, Labor has, at times, had the *power* to exercise freedom of association. So the question we confront today is: Given all our history, *what do we want the next National Labor Relations Act to look like?*

RIGHTS-BASED MOVEMENT, RIGHTS-BASED LAW

For starters, a new National Labor Relations Act must be rooted in the First Amendment, which guarantees freedom of speech, assembly and association, and in the Thirteenth Amendment, which abolished slavery and involuntary servitude. It should also draw on the Fourteenth Amendment, which guaranteed equal protection under the law.

But a new Labor Act must go further. It must throw out Taft-Hartley and bring back Norris-LaGuardia, because in order to be free, people must be able to exercise freedom of speech and assembly, *in the workplace* and *in the community*. They must have the right to organize and the right to support the ideas and the people that promote their needs and aspirations. They must have the right to boycott those who would attack their rights and diminish their quality of life.

Based on the Amendments cited above, the right to representation in the employment setting is self-evident. If a person at work is denied the protection of the First and Fourteenth Amendments, namely free speech and due process, the employer has placed the worker in a condition of involuntary servitude, which violates the 13th Amendment.

Put another way, it is assumed that we will have a Congress; the only question we vote on is the choice of who will represent us. Similarly, the assumption in the workplace is that the worker is in the condition of involuntary servitude if no representation is present. You can't have *freedom* without *labor organization and representation*.

The present National Labor Relations Act is rooted in the Commerce Clause of the Constitution. It is basically a subset of the clause that protects and promotes the interests of employers. The new law must be grounded in human rights, not corporate privilege. The Federal Government must pass a law giving workers an explicit right to organize in their workplace.

Along with guaranteeing workers the right to organize, the law should include health and safety provisions which the employer must meet. And while ensuring a safe, healthy work environment, the law should also require the employer to maintain a healthy environment in the surrounding habitats which may be degraded by the company's operations.

Will it be hard to pass a new labor law based on human rights? Indeed, it will a long, tough uphill slog. But as Samuel Gompers said:

> History honors none above those who, in the past, have set themselves against unjust laws, even unto the point of rebellion. The Republic of the United States is founded upon defiance of unjust law...manifestly unjust decisions of courts must be defied...[1]

It was the militant labor activities of the 1930s, including the general strikes and mass sit-downs, that brought about the passage and implementation of the National Labor Relations Act. It will take a struggle of similar proportions on the part of workers — a struggle that once again defies the authority of the courts and the corporations — to rebuild our unions and bring about a new labor law.

It will be a law that puts into practice the lofty ideals that are expressed in the Constitution but were crushed by the laws of property and contract that robbed workers of their rights and hobbled their ability to organize against their oppressor.

FOOTNOTES

Part 1: The Problem

1 U.S. Bureau of Labor Statistics, Union Members Summary, USDL-25-0105 1/28/2025.

Part 2: Knowing Our History

1 Zeese Papanikolas, <u>Buried Unsung - Louis Tikas and the Ludlow Massacre</u> (University of Nebraska Press, 1991), p. 259.
2 Charles A. Beard, <u>An Economic Interpretation of the Constitution of the United States</u> (New York: Free Press, 1986), p. 144. "Washington of Virginia was probably the richest man in the United States in his time, and his financial ability was not surpassed among his countrymen anywhere."
3 Willard Randall, <u>George Washington - A Life</u> (New York: Henry Holt & Co, 1997), p. 68.
4 Bruce Levine [et. al.], <u>Who Built America,</u> Vol. 1 (New York: Pantheon Books, 1989), p. 25.
5 Jerry Fresia, <u>Toward an American Revolution</u> (Boston: South End Press, 1988), p. 26. See also Abbot Emerson Smith's <u>Colonists in Bondage - White Servitude and Convict Labor in America, 1607-1776</u> (Baltimore: Genealogical Co., 1998), p. 336.
6 <u>Who Built America,</u> Vol. 1, p. 105.
7 *Minor v. Happersett*, 88 U.S.162 (1875), p. 172-73.
8 Francis N. Thorpe, <u>The Story of the Constitution of the United States</u>. (New York: Chautauqua Press, 1891), p. 48.
9 Charles Beard, <u>The Republic-Conversations on Fundamentals</u> (New York: Viking Press, 1943), p. 285.
10 Charles Beard, Ibid, p. 285
11 Charles Beard, Ibid, p. 287

Part 3: Corporations and The Constitution

1 Elsie W. Clews, <u>Educational Legislation and Administration of the Colonial Governments</u> (New York: Macmillan, 1899), p. 171.
2 Clews, p. 173.
3 For a more detailed discussion of the Dartmouth College case, see articles by the author in *By What Authority:* "You Have Heard of Santa Clara, Now Meet Dartmouth," Vol. 2, No.2, Spring 2000, and "Public or Private," Vol. 2, No. 3, Summer 2000, published by The Program on Corporations, Law and Democracy, P.O. Box 246, South Yarmouth, MA 02664-0246
4 *Minor v. Happersett*, 88 U.S.162 (1875).
5 William B. Forbath, *Law and the Shaping of the American Labor Movement* (Cambridge: Harvard University Press, 1991), p. 38
6 Leon Fink, "Labor, Liberty and the Law: Trade Unionism and the Problem of the American Constitutional Order," <u>In Search of the Working Class: Essays in American Labor History</u>

and Political Culture (Urbana: University of Illinois Press, 1994), p. 150.

7 Philip S. Foner, *The Great Labor Uprising of 1877* (New York: Pathfinder, 1977), p. 15

8 Jeremy Brecher, *Strike!* (Boston: South End Press, 1980), p. 1.

Part 4: Labor Stands Up

1 Who Built America, Vol. 2, p. 116.

2 Charles A. Scontras, Samuel Gompers and the American Federation of Labor vs. Maine's Congressman Charles E. Littlefield, 1900-1913 (Orono, Maine: Bureau of Labor education, 1998, p.8

3 John Mitchell, Organized Labor (Philadelphia: American Book and Bible House 1903, p. 324)

4 Samuel Gompers, "Union Labor and the Enlightened Employer," 28 American Federalist 469-472 (1921).

5 *American Federation of Labor History Encyclopedia Reference Book* (Washington, D.C., 1919) P.254

6 Ralph Chaplin, Bars and Shadows (Ridgewood, N.J.: Nellie Seeds Nearing, 1922).

7 Howard Zinn, "Eugene V. Debs and the Idea of Socialism," *The Progressive*, Jan. 1999, p. 16.

Part 5: Labor Wins and Loses

1 Leon Fink, "Labor, Liberty, and the Law: Trade Unionism and the Problem of the American Constitutional Order" in In Search of the American Working Class: Essays in American Labor History and Political Culture (Urbana: University of Illinois Press, 1994), p. 251. Also, between 1880 and 1931 judges issued 1800 injunctions against strikes (*ibid*).

2 "Yellow dog contracts" are contracts that individual workers are required to sign stating that the worker will never join a union.

3 Norris-LaGuardia does not prevent state courts from issuing injunctions in labor disputes. However, by 1941, 24 states had anti-injunction laws. See Harry Millis and Royal Montgomery, Organized Labor (New York: McGraw-Hill, 1945), p. 647.

4 *National Labor Relations Board v. Mackay Radio* - 304 U.S. 333 (1938); *National Labor Relations Board v. Virginia Electric & Power Co.* – 314 U.S. 469, (1941).

5 Leo Troy, Trade Union Membership, 1897-1962, (New York: National Bureau of Economic Research, 1965

6 Report of U.S. Department of Labor's Bureau of Labor Statistics, Jan. 2001.

Part 6: Labor's Future

1 Samuel Gompers, "The Courts and Mr. Taft on Labor," 28 *American Federationist* 220, 222 (1921).

Peter Kellman is an organizer, writer/researcher and teacher.

He has been an activist for the past 60 years involved in the Civil rights and anti-war movements of the 1960s, the anti-nuclear movement of the 1970s and organized labor from the 1970s to the present.

He is an active member of the United Auto Workers Union and works with the Maine AFL-CIO on new projects.

Kellman has published three books and is past president of a shoe workers local, executive board member of the Maine AFL-CIO and President Emeritus of the Southern Maine Labor Council.

He is best know for his role in the 1987-'88 strike by Local 14 of the United Paperworkers International Union against the International Paper Company.

Matt Wuerker is a political cartoonist for and founding staff member of Politico and winner of the 2012 Pulitzer Prize for Editorial Cartooning. He has been awarded the 2010 Herblock Prize by the Library of Congress. The National Press Foundation chose him for the 2010 Clifford K. and James T. Berryman Award for editorial cartooning, one the field's most prestigious awards. Berryman Award by.

Matt has published two collections of cartoons, *Standing Tall in Deep Doo Doo, A Cartoon Chronicle of the Bush Quayle Years* (Thunder's Mouth Press, 1991) and *Meanwhile in Other News... A Graphic Look at Politics in the Empire of Money, Sex and Scandal* (Common Courage Press, 1998). He illustrated the book The Madness of King George (Common Courage Press, 2003) by Michael K. Smith.

MORE TITLES FROM HARD BALL PRESS

A Great Vision: A Militant Family's Journey Through the Twentieth Century, Richard March

A Pandemic Nurse's Journal, Nurse T with Tim Sheard

The Activist Spirit: Toward a Radical Solidarity, Victor Narro

The Art of Organizing, Michael Raysson

Asian Workers Stories, Luka Lei Zhang, editor

Caring: 1199 Nursing Home Workers Tell Their Story, Tim Sheard, ed.

Good Trouble, Steve Thornton

Fight For Your Long Day, Classroom Edition, Alex Kudera

I Just Got Elected, Now What? Bill Barry

I Still Can't Fly: Confessions of a Lifelong Troublemaker, Kevin John Carroll

Legacy Costs, Richard Hudelson

Love Dies, A Thriller, Timothy Sheard

The Man Who Changed Colors, Bill Fletcher

The Man Who Fell From the Sky, Bill Fletcher Jr.

Murder of a Post Office Manager, A Legal Thriller, Paul Felton

New York Hustle: Pool Rooms, School Rooms and Street Corner, Stan Maron

Presente: A Dockworker Story, Herb Mills

Radical Connecticut: People's History In The Constitution State, Steve Thornton & Andy Piascik

Sixteen Tons, A Novel, Kevin Corley

Standing Up: Tales of Struggle, Ellen Bravo & Larry Miller

Throw Out the Water, Kevin Corley

Union Made, Ertic Lotke

What Did You Learn at Work Today? The Forbidden Lessons of Labor Education, Helena Worthen

With Our Loving Hands: 1199 Nursing Home Workers Tell Their Story

Winning Richmond: How a Progressive Alliance Won City Hall, Gayle McLaughlin

Woman Missing, A Mill Town Mystery, Linda Nordquist

www.ingramcontent.com/pod-product-compliance
Lightning Source LLC
Chambersburg PA
CBHW081726120626
46550CB00010B/3266